SECOND CAREERS
for STREET COPS

John Eldridge

for LORI

Copyright 2015 by John Eldridge

No part of this book may be reproduced in any form or by any electronic or mechanical means including information storage and retrieval systems, without permission in writing from the author. The only exception is by a reviewer, who may quote short excerpts in a review.

All rights reserved.

Edited by Molly McKitterick, The Word Process
Book design and cover by Edward Wong, Vertex Design
First Printing April 2015

Contents

Introduction

CHAPTER 1   11
Before Your Investigation - The Value of a Police Career

CHAPTER 2   21
Assess the Situation

CHAPTER 3   29
Gather the Facts

CHAPTER 4   47
Identify a Person of Interest

CHAPTER 5   57
Describe this Person of Interest

CHAPTER 6   65
Fill the Gaps in Your Investigation

CHAPTER 7   75
Record of Investigation

CHAPTER 8 — 83
Every Investigation Needs an Operational Plan – Design Yours

CHAPTER 9 — 89
Follow-up. Looking Ahead

CHAPTER 10 — 95
Second Career Stories. From Street Cop to …

Recommended Reading — 101

Index — 105

Acknowledgments — 109

Introduction

This book is for street cops who are looking ahead to a second career. It's also for retired street cops who may be feeling they want to try one more career before full retirement.

A second career for street cops isn't that unusual anymore. I know. I'm a former police officer who's had a second career. Many others have too. For some, a second career has become a necessity.

After serving with the Vancouver Police Department for 26 years, I moved on to a successful second career at WorkSafeBC that lasted 11 years. I started there as the Manager of Field Investigations right after my police career. Our section investigated fraud and misrepresentation. Then I took over as the Manager of Fatal and Serious Injury Investigations. Just as it sounds, we investigated workplace fatalities and serious accidents.

And it was skills that I developed from my police career that got me those jobs. As you'll see from the stories in *Second Careers for Street Cops,* those policing skills got a lot of other street cops their second careers too.

That's where this book comes in. To help you make that transition.

How? By capitalizing on the unique skill set developed in your street policing experience. And not just in the obvious areas of investigations and security. Lots of street cops follow those paths for a second career. But as you'll see from the stories in this book, they do many other things too.

The book will help you move forward to a second career. It will take you through the steps of self-evaluation and look at what the work world outside of policing values in police experience. *Second Careers for Street Cops* will give you some new ideas about putting together a resumé. Then you'll design a customized operational plan, just for you.

And it won't cost you a lot of money.

Second Careers for Street Cops is written in language familiar to police officers. It deals with the particular job experiences unique to policing.

The book follows a pattern you would be familiar with in conducting an investigation. It begins with looking at the value of the investigation. That's followed by an assessment of your situation, then a gathering of the known facts. The facts are analyzed and a report gets written. An operational plan is designed for your next steps. Then you look ahead to future possibilities.

Like this….

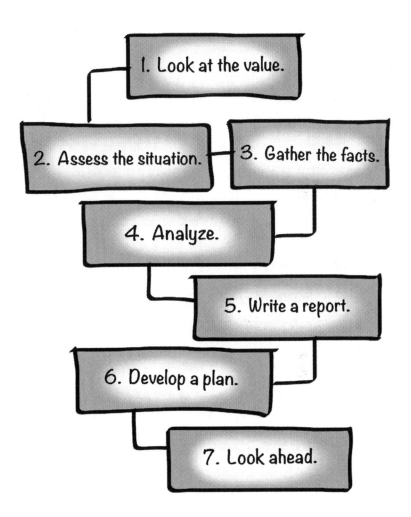

Diagram by Brad Hill

Why bother doing all this now? You could just wait until your police career ends and then plan for a second career. However this is your chance to look ahead while there is no pressure to bring all your information together in a hurry.

If you want a second career, take the time now to organize your police career profile, put together a resumé, and develop a plan. That way, if an opportunity presents itself, you'll be ready. And you won't have missed any important details that would help you put your best foot forward.

The alternative is scrambling to put something together in a short period of time. Just try to remember overnight all the great things you learned in your entire police career. Something will get missed.

You might be thinking, "Why in the world would I want another career after what I've been through as a street cop? I'm done." Fair enough. If that's you, put this book back on the shelf and break out the golf clubs. You've earned it.

But if it's not you, and you want some new challenges, here's a way to approach those challenges with a plan that will put you in the best possible position for success.

Courtesy of JohnPWeiss.com

CHAPTER 1

Before Your Investigation - The Value of a Police Career

Jack Ewatski was a police officer in Winnipeg for 34 years and the Chief of Police for nine of those. Here is what he had to say about the value of a police career:

"I think police officers undervalue themselves in terms of their experience, skills, and training. Consider all the skills they have in conflict resolution, problem solving and stress management. An officer should try to keep that in mind. Some say 'all I know is policing' when they finish their police careers but they really need to stop and think about all the skills they've learned that are valued by employers. There are all sorts of positions out there."

This chapter is about the skills you've learned as a police officer.

Consider the skills used in this typical police incident. It was an assignment many street cops are familiar with. On a busy Friday night in Vancouver during the Christmas season a call came into the police communications center asking for help at a family dispute.

The call-taker noted lots of shouting in the background during the phone call. It sounded like pandemonium. And it sounded urgent.

Only one unit was available. The dispatcher sent that officer the call and he responded.

The officer arrived at the address the call had come from, parked his patrol car, and approached the house. The drapes in the living room were open and he could see four or five people standing around.

He did a quick assessment of the situation. There wasn't any shouting or loud noise coming from the house. Things seemed to have calmed down.

He decided to ring the door bell and see if the police were still needed.

As the officer walked up to the front door, he saw a quick movement in the living room out of the corner of his eye and the Christmas turkey came crashing through the front window…

What to do? Keep going and get inside to see what was going on? He was on his own. He needed backup but all the other units were still busy. Someone inside may have needed help urgently. What to make of the turkey coming through the window? He wasn't sure but knew it wasn't good.

He knocked hard on the door.

Fortunately, other officers arrived just then to back him up. They entered the house together and the situation was brought under control.

The skills

Let's look at the skills that officer used. Consider the quick thinking he had to use as he figured out a course of action. In the short time he was there, he processed the known facts and assessed a potentially dangerous situation. Then he used his judgment as to whether or not to enter the house. This was followed by decision-making and problem confrontation as he knocked on the door. Throughout this situation he had to remain mindful of the law and policies of the police department.

All this was done quickly on a dark and cold December night out on the street, not in a warm office with lots of time to think and come to a decision about the best course of action. Who else does that! It's a remarkable skill set developed and refined under the most adverse conditions. And these are only a very few of the skills a street cop uses during a routine shift.

There are few careers that can match policing for the kind of dynamic experiences future employers value.

Think about it. Street cops all over the world have valuable skills. You're one of them. You know about risks, problem solving, using good judgment, decision-making, taking action, and much more. A lot of your work is carried out under very difficult conditions.

There are always public disorder issues to deal with. Bank robbers, thieves, drunks and drug addicts, street cops see them all on a daily basis. The human drama gets played out before you in ways other people never see.

You're often the first helpful contact many unfortunate people have when things go wrong, a problem solver when there's no one else to call.

Then there are the death investigations. Think about the empathy and tact required to properly deliver a death notification. Street cops do it all the time. How many careers deal with death as much as street cops do? And what does that experience mean in terms of skills and experience?

It means you have a unique skill set to offer future employers.

What would a future employer think?

You have experience making order out of chaos, and can deal with people in the most difficult predicaments. You get the job done under the most trying circumstances. You have the ability to think on your feet.

Not everyone can do all this! These skills are valuable. So are the many technical skills you learned in police work. For example, gathering information, making concise notes, processing a crime scene, seizing evidence, photography skills, and report writing are all useful in other settings.

Employers recognize a wide range of skills learned in police work that can help their organizations.

In my own police career, as the years passed, I had more and more valuable exposure to difficult challenges. By the end, I had a good portfolio of experience and skills learned as a police officer.

You will too. All you have to do is organize them and develop a plan.

Transferable skills

Street cops everywhere use these skills in a lot of different and unpredictable situations. And they're transferable skills. You can put them to good use in many different second careers.

Kevin McQuiggin was a police officer for 30 years. When he retired from policing, he moved on to a position as a Second Officer flying DC10 cargo planes.

Kevin had developed an interest in flying at age 42, midway in his police career. He got his private pilot's license and went on to become a flying instructor.

Thinking ahead to a second career, he continued to work on his flying skills and qualifications, eventually becoming certified to fly jet aircraft. At age 52 he was hired by an air charter firm and began his second career as a professional pilot.

Kevin developed a love of flying and looked ahead to a second career. He said: "I didn't want to be 60 years old and think I could have been a pilot but didn't do it."

He included his police skills in his resumé when applying for a position as a pilot and emphasized his experience staying calm under pressure. As Kevin said, "I didn't panic when I was at a 'man with a gun' call in police work. I used that experience to explain I wouldn't panic if there was an engine fire or some other serious problem in the aircraft."

Kevin's advice to street cops considering a second career is to have a plan. He recommends those looking ahead to "invest in your future. Spend some money."

Kevin believes in learning and training for your second career while you're still in your police career.

Jim Padar was a Chicago police officer for 29 years. He worked as a patrol officer, tactical officer, homicide detective, sergeant and lieutenant. When Jim finished his police career he went on to a second career as Operations Manager for the 911 system in the City of Chicago.

Toward the end of his police career, Jim was assigned to the training section. He was responsible for producing multi-media presentations. He'd also had a background in engineering and an interest in an early 911 system at the beginning of his police career. Jim was getting ready to retire from the Chicago PD and, when the position at the 911 system came open, he was ready to go. Building on his engineering background, his work in multi-media, and his police management experience, he applied for the job. It became a natural move for him from policing to the operations manager position.

Jim also co-authored a book with his son Jay Padar, a Chicago police sergeant. Their book, *On Being A Cop*, is a collection of 53 stories about life as a Chicago street cop. They're told with emotional, heart-thumping, palms sweating clarity. Want an insight into fighting crime on the streets of Chicago? Read *On Being A Cop*. If you're a street cop you'll relate to the wild and bizarre situations described in the book. And if you're just a reader of good police stories, the book will keep you intrigued, entertained, and laughing at the sometimes comical situations they came across.

In the About the Authors section of their book, Jim and Jay described how they wrote it: "*On Being a Cop* was born when Jay first hit the streets of Chicago as a rookie cop. Like most new cops, he would arrive home after a midnight tour of duty, his residual adrenaline not conducive to sleep, so he started writing emails to his dad, chronicling the night's experiences. Dad read and smiled with pride and admiration – his son was capturing in writing the wonder of being a new cop, but more than that, Jay wrote with soul and a sensitivity seldom seen in police stories. "Keep writing son," he emailed back. 'For every story you write, I'll write one.'"

This was the beginning of another second career for Jim. Or perhaps we should call it his third career. He combined his long interest in writing, his 29-year police career, and son Jay's strong writing interest. All these aspects of Jim's life came together, enabling him to transition into another fulfilling career as an author.

Jim encourages police officers to try a variety of assignments throughout their police career. His advice is: "Move around. Do some different jobs. One of them might be your second career."

I hope by now you're becoming convinced of the great skill set you've acquired during your police career.

Adaptable skills

I spent eleven years in my second career at WorkSafeBC. During that time I managed a team that investigated workplace fatalities and serious injuries. I hired a lot of investigators, most of whom had policing as a background.

Those police officers I hired had widely different backgrounds. All had spent considerable time on the street. Some had specialized later in their careers. But none had in-depth knowledge of investigations specific to workplace accidents.

It didn't matter. They were all able to adapt easily to those types of investigations. They simply used the skills and knowledge they'd learned as police officers and applied them to investigating workplace fatalities and serious injury accidents.

You can do this

You can do the same thing. Your police career is a valuable asset, one that you can put to good use in a second career. All you have to do is adapt your skills to a new set of circumstances. Take all that you've learned and adapt it to a different employment environment. Yes, it's challenging, but lots of your fellow officers have done it.

It's never too late

I'm making the assumption that you're well into your police career and know quite a lot about yourself. This book isn't intended for someone who is just starting into a police career. It's for those street cops who have been at it for awhile and are looking ahead to the end of their police careers.

And for you retired street cops who might be thinking it's too late to start something new, don't let the passing years get in the way of trying one more career. Just make it something you're going to really enjoy. You've earned that. As Karen Schaffer noted in her book *The Job of Your Life*, "There is no too late. It's only too late when you're dead." See Recommended Reading for more information about Karen's book.

As you work through the chapters of *Second Careers for Street Cops*, keep in mind there is not one definitive set of skills that will fit every second career. However, by the end of the book you should be able to see what skills and experience match your personal police profile, what the possibilities are for a second career, and where the gaps in your profile are.

One of my proudest moments was when I landed the job at WorkSafeBC to start my second career. Think about how you'll feel when another organization recognizes your skills and experience and hires you. It's a great feeling and something for you to look forward to as you do your preparation.

CHAPTER 2

Assess the Situation

One of the first things I learned when I started training in the police academy was to "assess the situation." The idea was this: Wherever you are or whatever situations you get into, before you plunge ahead size up the situation and figure out a plan.

You can apply these same principles when considering a second career. This chapter will show you how to assess your present situation as you begin to look ahead to a second career.

Consider this scenario.

We crept down the stairs into the basement suite. Two street cops in uniform, there to make the arrest. The suspect was alone, or so we thought.

He was sitting in a chair asleep. Good thing. He was huge. My partner slipped the handcuffs on him quickly. All of a sudden he awoke and stood up like a big grizzly bear.

At that very moment his drugged up, passed out, girlfriend popped up from behind a couch and screamed: "What are you doing?" Then she started throwing things at us. She had our attention for the instant it took buddy in handcuffs to grab a kitchen chair and start swinging it with both hands. All hell broke loose ….

Looking back at that experience, you could argue we didn't do a very good assessment of what we were facing when we got in there. And you'd be right. The result was pandemonium and flying furniture. We got out of it ok but not without some very anxious moments. It could have gone really badly if we weren't able to regain control of the situation. It happens.

The same is true of your plans for a second career. Without a good assessment and development of a plan, you could easily end up with the second career version of our wild and chaotic situation.

> Tip #1: Spend some focused time thinking about it.

Self-Reflection

This may seem obvious. But just in case you want to jump straight to the planning stage, know that it takes some reflection and self-assessment to figure out what you want before developing a plan.

We'll get to a detailed self-assessment later. First though, when I was thinking about moving on from my police career to something different, I went back to basics and simply sat down and thought about it.

Sounds simple, but like many police officers, I'm not one to sit and reflect for long periods of time. I much prefer working and getting things done.

This time I made myself sit back and think about where I wanted to go in life.

I was about 50 at that time. I knew whatever I chose

for a second career had to be something I would enjoy. I wanted to keep working at something I liked so I thought long and hard about my next career step.

I asked myself: "What kind of work do I want to do?"

It's really a loaded question in the sense that it made me think about a lot of things. Like my own personal value system, how it would impact my family, where I wanted to live, and how much I expected to be paid. Then there was the big question of the work itself and what I would actually be doing each time I went to work.

Reality check

What's the reality of your situation? You may have family responsibilities and a mortgage. Perhaps you have some financial moves to recover from. In a second family? That's common in the police community. The job can be hard on relationships. Do you want full-time work or part-time? Everyone has their own individual circumstances. Think what you'd do in a perfect world. Now look at your own reality.

Start with that. Make a few notes. Think about:

- What kind of work you want to do;

___

___

___

___

___

- And when you want to do it ...When would you make the move to a second career?

___

Chapter Four will present you with some other ideas for reflecting on what skills you bring to a second career. The two questions above are just the basics, ideas to give you a beginning for some further analysis.

What would you really like to do?

The most obvious second career for street cops would probably be one similar to policing, such as an investigations job or the security business. Great choices if that's what you have in mind. However that may not be what you want and before you simply go with the obvious take some time to assess what you would really like to do.

While you're assessing your situation, why not think about your dream job?

This whole book is about creating options for you, getting yourself into the best possible position to make choices about your future. Why get locked into one second career stream unless you really want to? If your second career is years away you have time to think and plan.

Kevin McQuiggin found his dream job after more than twenty-nine years in policing when he became a professional pilot. He assessed his situation and planned ahead while he was still enjoying his police career. You can too.

> Tip #2: Pay attention to your reputation.

Your reputation

As part of assessing your situation, think about your reputation. It's a fundamental part of your career foundation and, to some extent, is already in place.

Whether you're interviewing a suspect, writing a police report, giving evidence in court, or carrying out any of the wide range of activities that make up a typical shift in policing, you're building your reputation.

Assess your reputation. No matter what qualities you say you bring to a potential employer, they won't mean much if you have a reputation that spells trouble to a new organization. And don't forget your reputation in the broader community, beyond your police reputation.

Was that your name showing up in the news media regarding the latest big policing scandal? If that's your reality, you probably want to consider how you might deal with questions about that at a future job interview. Potential employers do reference checks and know how to search the internet.

Social media

Assess your personal social media sites. Consider what you want to share with anyone who views them. That picture of you at your unit party with a beer in your hand and a lamp shade on your head may not create a positive impression for a future employer.

PROTECT YOUR ONLINE REPUTATION

Courtesy of JohnPWeiss.com

There's a very concise article on the PoliceOne.com website called *5 great ways to destroy your police career on social media* by former police chief Dr. Richard Weinblatt. The issues he points out are the same ones that could destroy your chances for future employment.

People Talk

When I was hiring investigators at WorkSafeBC to investigate fatal accidents in the workplace, I did a lot of reference checks. I was sometimes surprised at what the applicant's references told me.

Applicants name people as references who will offer positive comments about them. However, as you know from your experience in police work, people like to talk, and once they start talking, sometimes they say the most surprising things...

And they aren't always positive. It all comes down to reputation though and, even if there are some negative comments, a good reputation often overcomes them.

Your reputation is a powerful force. Chris Komisarjevsky retired as worldwide chief executive officer of Burson-Marsteller, one of the world's leading global public relations and public affairs firms. He had this to say in his book, *The Power of Reputation:*

"Reputation is very powerful and it is crucial to success, whether you are measured by the way people perceive you or by the results you reach. A strong reputation — built on character, communication, and trust – is the foundation for lasting success." See more about *The Power of Reputation* in Recommended Reading.

You were selected to become a police officer because of the personal characteristics you demonstrated when you were hired. High integrity, hard work, and reliability are just a few of the many characteristics that make up a good reputation.

You've built your reputation as you progressed through your police career. It will follow you into your search for a second career. Keep it intact, and make it your greatest asset.

Now that you've assessed your situation and considered some aspects of moving to a second career, Chapter Three will help you begin to organize a portfolio of your police career.

CHAPTER 3

Gather the Facts

This chapter is where you collect all your police career experience in one place and make sure you haven't missed anything.

We'll break it all down into your career building blocks. That will make it easier when you're extracting what you've learned.

Cartoon by Brad Hill

Give all your records a good review and write down as much information as you can remember. Once you're satisfied that you've done that, you'll be ready to move on to the next chapter and start analyzing your police career.

Don't be concerned about your skills, strengths, weaknesses, etc. at this point. The building blocks are just an easy way to record where you've worked. Get it all organized into one place. The analysis comes later.

Your big assignments:

I had some really interesting assignments during my police career. I worked undercover for a long period of time, disappearing from the camaraderie and familiarity of the police department for months. When the project ended, I went back to wearing a police uniform and driving a marked police car. It was hard to get out of the undercover role. I got over it, but the transition back to normal police duties took a while.

I learned a lot about crime and criminals during that time working undercover. It gave me a deeper understanding of how crooks think and operate. Years later, when I was in police management, I drew on that undercover experience many times when making decisions about police deployment and investigations.

Toward the end of my police career I had a really satisfying assignment. The police department was moving to a new building and I was part of the team assigned to coordinate and organize the move.

Part of our job was to furnish the new police station with everything from furniture to equipment. Our patrol officers were all going to get new lockers when we moved into the new building. We needed to know what kind of lockers to purchase and what the interior design of the lockers should look like.

Up to that time our officers had been using the standard, narrow, high school style lockers. One of my jobs was to find out what kind of lockers to buy for our new police station

I decided the best way to approach this project was to assemble a group of patrol officers and see if we could figure out together what style of locker to buy. I found twelve patrol officers willing to take part in the discussion and we brainstormed as a group.

The officers weren't shy about what they wanted. No surprise there. Street cops are good at letting you know what they think.

They had very definite ideas about how to improve the lockers they used. One of the main improvements they wanted was more ways to hang equipment and clothing inside the locker. This was especially important to the officers. Their equipment and uniforms are often wet when they put them away at the end of a shift. Letting their uniforms hang freely with some extra ventilation would help them dry quicker.

We had several meetings and worked together at drawing a model of what the interior of the lockers would look like. After lots of discussion, we settled on the locker we wanted for the new police station.

The patrol officers were fully consulted through the process and had plenty of opportunity to put their ideas forward. They were pleased with the improvements provided by the new lockers. It was a win-win for all involved.

The project was a great learning experience for me. I learned a lot about groups working together to solve a problem, improved my listening skills, and found out what excellent results can occur when all parties feel like they have been heard.

The experience and skills I learned from that assignment stayed with me. I continued to develop my work strengths and never forgot what I learned on that project. The things I learned were valuable when I moved into my second career.

You've also had significant assignments and accomplishments. Record them as you work through this chapter. We'll look at the skills you learned later.

Before you get into this, dig out all your diplomas, certificates, commendations, professional designation letters, and awards, anything that you might want to include in building your career profile.

Cartoon by Brad Hill

Don't forget any recognition you've had from volunteer positions.

As you record your career building blocks, make sure you use the correct titles. (That's why you need to dig them out. It's too hard to remember exactly how some of them are worded.)

Ask your Human Relations or Training Department for a copy of your training record. You can use that to help you recall every police training course you've taken.

Block A: Your Foundation

Part of your foundation is your life before policing, so list your academic and training accomplishments. Include languages you are fluent in and cultural diversity expertise. Note other special skills.

Include your employment experience prior to policing.

Now get into the start of your police career. Describe your police academy training or whatever program you went through to qualify you as a working street cop. List the courses and practical training you took in that program.

For example, your Block A list may read like this:

Graduated _____ High School in 1992.

Employed before police career as a landscaper.

Speak two languages beside English: French and Spanish.

Completed two-year diploma in Police Studies at _____ College in 1996.

Joined _____ PD September 16, 1996

Police academy training at _____ Police Academy from September, 1996 to October, 1997.

Police Academy study topics included legal studies, patrol tactics, report writing, firearms qualification, police driving, etc.

Write your list here.

Block B: First Assignments

This block is the first part of your police career after academy training. Usually it's general patrol experience and can last any number of years, depending on many variables. Often, it's the first five to ten years of a police career.

Think back to some of the unique experiences you had during this period, special projects or events you were involved in. Include seminars, workshops, and any specialized training.

For example, after a period of time in patrol, you may have been given the opportunity to take an advanced investigations course or community problem solving course. Perhaps there were high profile incidents in your jurisdiction that required you to participate in specialized training such as crowd control. There are many possibilities. No two street cops will have exactly the same training or experience to make note of.

Your Block B might look something like this:

Graduated from police academy, October 24, 1997.

Assigned to Patrol Division, Zone 9, 1997 to 2003.

General patrol duties.

Assigned to Narcotics Squad Task Force, November 1999 to February, 2000.

Assigned to Summer Beach Patrol, May to September, 2001.

Attended Advanced Patrol Officers Training Program in September, 2000. One month.

Received Chief's Commendation for bank robber arrest, March, 2002.

Attended three-day community problem-solving seminar, January, 2003.

Transferred to Traffic Division, August, 2003.

And so on ….

Block C: After Patrol

Now recall your other assignments and training beyond patrol work over the years. Think about any advanced training courses you took.

You may have begun to specialize during this part of your career, so record areas you worked in and the technical skills you learned. There is a long list of possibilities here.

For example, you could have become a dog handler, a detective, or a news media specialist representing your police agency. Perhaps you joined the Emergency Response Team or a specialized investigations unit. Any such assignments would have probably included a training program. Customize this block to your own unique experience.

List all the places you have worked in your police agency after your time in patrol. List all the police training courses you took.

Include relevant training outside of your police career. Perhaps you pursued further education during this time.

(Remember, all you need to do in this chapter is make lists of your training and experience. The analysis of your skills comes later.)

_____

_____

_____

_____

Block D: Supervisory experience

This is where you record your supervisory experience. You may have been the lead officer on a particular file or project. Were you a field training officer or mentor to junior officers? Perhaps you're a sergeant at this point with a squad you're responsible for.

List your supervisory assignments. Include all police supervisory training.

Include any supervisory training taken outside your police agency. Some street cops, anticipating that they will one day compete for a supervisory position, take courses on their own time to expand their knowledge base and credentials. List them here.

_____

_____

_____

_____

_____

_____

_____

_____

_____

_____

_____

_____

(This may seem like a lot of work and tedious but hang in there. You only have to do this work once. Then it's just a matter of adding new items or updating from time to time. We'll cover that later in the book.)

Block E: Police management experience

Perhaps after all your street cop experience, you moved into police management. Record your police leadership and management training.

Include your police management experience, both operational and administrative.

Courtesy of JohnPWeiss.com

Block F: Volunteer experience

Don't overlook the valuable experience that comes from being a volunteer. Street cops volunteer their time to support their communities in many ways.

The volunteer work can sometimes be just as challenging as paid employment. There are many lessons to be learned from this experience. Often, there are training programs for volunteers.

Many police officers volunteer time in support of their police union. This gives them a broader perspective on policing.

Some senior police union members represent other officers in the discipline process and learn valuable skills in doing so. Others serve as executive members of the union, developing excellent knowledge of labor and management issues. Consider the critical skills required in being part of a team negotiating a collective agreement.

I have personally known three police chiefs who held executive positions in their respective police unions during their careers. Obviously, they made good use of the experience, developing important skills during that time.

List your volunteer training and experience.

Block G: The "anything else" block

I put this box in because police agencies are so diverse and different. It really isn't possible to design building blocks that fit all police experiences.

You may be part of a very large police organization or a very small one. You may police in a rural area or surrounded by high rise buildings. Each police agency has its own unique characteristics. There might be some training or experience that doesn't fit in one of the other blocks.

This is also your overflow box, the place to record any special experiences you haven't included so far.

For example, remember the time you attended that six-car motor vehicle accident? You arranged for medical treatment, coordinated access around the accident scene, and sorted out who was driving each vehicle. Then you figured out who was at fault, and wrote a report.

Well, that shows you have a number of skills that are transferable to other jobs. If you enjoyed that kind of work, you must be good at making order out of chaos, a talent that can be useful in many ways.

List any special, unique experiences and skills that you haven't recorded to this point.

_____
_____
_____
_____
_____
_____
_____
_____

Moving on to your analysis:

You've gathered all your information. These are your work-life building blocks, all stacked in one place. This is what you will build on as you plan for your second career. For example, I wrote this book by building on my police career and then my second career. Go forward from here, building on what you have achieved so far.

> Tip #3: Build, build, build. Build on who you are and what you know.

Pause here to consider whether or not you have gathered every piece of information you will use to build the platform for your second career. This is an important feature of launching a second career so it's important to include everything of value.

Martin Yate is one of the foremost experts in the field of job search and career management. He had this to say about gathering your information in his book *Knock'em Dead Resumes*:

"Take Your Time: You're laying the foundation for career success. It may be tempting to rush through it or look for shortcuts, but remember that you're assembling the information that's going to be the brick and mortar of your resumé, the most financially important document you are ever going to own. You need it to be as complete and well thought out as possible."

See more about *Knock'em Dead Resumes* in Recommended Reading.

Got everything listed? Good. Let's move on to an analysis of your police career.

CHAPTER 4

Identify a Person of Interest (That's You!) What are Your Strengths and Weaknesses? Examine Your Police Experience for Unique Skills and Talent

Now it's time to analyze, do some self-assessment, and discover what skills you have. This is an opportunity to focus your thinking and organize the results in a way that can be used later to develop your profile. (Your profile is simply a report you'll write about yourself.)

I've designed the chapter with a focus on the skills learned by street cops.

"Person of interest" is a broad and somewhat vague term. We use it when referring to someone who does not fall under the usual definitions found in police work.

A person of interest is not a victim, a suspect, an arrested or charged person. He/she is simply "of interest."

The "person of interest" in this book is you. You're going to investigate this person of interest.

In your work as a street cop, you make notes as you conduct investigations. Use this chapter like your notebook as you investigate this person of interest. Make your notes as you record your skills, strengths and weaknesses.

Now the great part about this is you're looking at YOUR police career and thinking about doing something just for YOU.

to know what you believe your
weaknesses are. For example,
that needs to know you're terrified
even if you do it well.

urself. You'll learn more that way
rofile that is really you.

Don't over-think it.

You can see by searching the internet or visiting the careers section of a bookstore, that there's an overwhelming amount of information available about careers, second careers, self-testing, and job-hunting.

It's easy to get lost in the vast amount of information on these topics. The result can be confusion and inertia. You can get stuck and not able to move forward. There's a danger of falling into this "paralysis by analysis" trap. You can analyze forever and never decide what you would like for a second career. Kind of like an investigator who turns over every rock in an investigation, to the point of complete irrelevance.

Hockey players sometimes get so focused on thinking about scoring that they can't put the puck in the net, no matter how good they are or how hard they try. Hockey analysts often say such players are over-thinking their scoring strategy rather than relying on their natural ability.

Let's not have that happen to you. Don't over-think your self-analysis. You're probably at a point in life where you have a pretty good idea what your talents are. Go with that. Rely on what you already know about yourself as you organize your profile.

One of the most challenging and interesting things I found about police work was that we often had a limited amount of time to gather information before something really bad was going to happen. We learned as much as we could about a situation, developed a plan, and decided on a course of action.

That's how I approach this kind of analysis.

If you decide you would like to do more in-depth analysis, perhaps with a broader focus, there are some good resources at the back of the book and on my website to help you.

Analyzing your police career

Going forward from here, you're going to create four lists about yourself: 1) Your Academic and Training Achievements, 2) The Skills You Acquired from your Experience, 3) Your Strengths and 4) Your Weaknesses. Make these lists by drawing on the experience and skills you noted in your building blocks.

Stay with me here. It's really quite a simple process:

Step 1 Go through each of your building blocks and note all your academic achievements, training courses, seminars. Make one list of all those and set that list aside. This is list #1.

_____

_____

_____

_____

_____

_____

_____

_____

> Tip #4: Get to know yourself really, really well.

Step 2 The next part requires more thought. Go through each of your building blocks to review all your assignments and experience. Note all the skills you learned in each building block.

There are many opportunities here to discover your skills and accomplishments. For instance, most police officers would be able to list problem confrontation as a starter. Then good judgment and decision making would follow. Other possibilities would be flexibility, mediation skills, and team work.

For example, perhaps you've been called to a neighbor/neighbor dispute, two neighbors yelling at each other over the back fence. The other residents of the area got disturbed, someone phoned the police, and you got the call. All pretty common stuff for street cops working in the patrol division.

Now think about the skills needed when you dealt with this incident. As you headed to the location, you gathered information about the participants. You had safety concerns, yours and that of other people in the neighborhood. You needed analytical skills as you approached the location and considered options.

On the scene, you used your assessment skills to grasp a quick understanding of what had been going on and what the present challenges were. You considered your use of force options, any laws that may have been broken and how to get things calmed down. You thought about making an arrest or giving a warning. But what would happen after you left? Would they start up again? You wanted to make sure that wouldn't happen.

You applied the law and policy of your police organization. Your mediation skills calmed the dispute. You looked for a way to resolve the problem that started the whole thing.

This is no desk job. Let's not forget the presence of mind needed at this and many other assignments you had. You used a variety of skills in dealing with the situation, all while operating under considerable stress, as usual.

This is just one example of the work of a street cop. There are many more. Consider the experiences you've had as you go through each building block. List all the skills you acquired.

Here's a partial list as an example. Depending on your own experience, you'll come up with a list unique to you.

- Problem confrontation
- Good judgment
- Decision-making
- Flexibility
- Assertiveness
- Mediation skills
- Teamwork
- Note-taking
- Oral communication
- Interviewing
- Written communication
- Crime scene preservation
- Crime scene investigation
- Accident investigation
- Seizing evidence
- Report writing
- Giving evidence
- Stress management
- Firearms proficiency
- Police driving
- Computer skills
- Presentation skills
- Photography skills
- Leadership skills
- anagement skills

r skills here. This is list #2.

_____
_____
_____
_____
_____
_____
_____
_____
_____
_____
_____
_____
_____

Step 3 Your strengths Now that we have your skills extracted from all of your police experience, we want to dig a little deeper and find your top three strengths. Later, when you're developing your ops plan, this may help you to discover what you want to do for a second career.

This is where you focus on your big strengths. What are you really good at?

One of the things I liked most during my police career was the teamwork aspect of the job. I played a lot of sports as a young guy and discovered I liked being part of a team.

The police department was one big team as far as I was concerned.

Later, when I was preparing for a second career, I listed "team player" as one of my strengths. Maybe this has been the same for you. If you enjoyed the working together aspect of policing, you're probably a good team player.

This is a good time to ask yourself what accomplishments in your police career you are proudest of. Thinking about those special achievements may lead you to identifying your big strengths.

List your top three strengths and note some times when you used these strengths. Write about why you enjoyed these experiences. This is list #3.

_____
_____
_____
_____
_____
_____
_____

Step 4 Your weaknesses Now let's look at your weaknesses. We've all got them. Don't forget, you're the only person who has to see this, so be completely honest with yourself. No one else needs to know.

What are the top three job skills that you have the most trouble with? Maybe you're a great investigator but struggle with writing reports. Perhaps you find it hard to present your evidence in court. Speaking to groups can be challenging, especially in situations such as giving evidence. Whatever you see as your down side, list your top three problem areas. This is list #4.

___

Now, you should have four lists resulting from your analysis.

- Your academic and training achievements,
- The skills you acquired from your experience,
- Your strengths and
- Your weaknesses.

It's time to write a report about this person of interest.

CHAPTER 5

Describe this Person of Interest. Start Organizing Your Profile

Let's review what you've done so far in organizing your career profile.

We began in Chapter One by thinking about how remarkable and valuable a police career is. Next, in Chapter Two, you assessed your situation and considered whether or not you wanted to plan for a second career. You thought about what that career might be. Then in Chapter Three, you reviewed the building blocks of your career. You listed all your achievements, training, and places you've worked in your police agency. In Chapter Four, you did some analysis and discovered your strengths and weaknesses.

Bring it all together

You've completed your investigation and made your notes. It's time to write a focused report about this person of interest. That's what this chapter is about. You'll write a report about yourself, this person of interest.

Up to now you've been using this book to make notes and lists. Your person of interest report should be written separately from this, somewhere you have enough room to include everything that needs to go in the report.

This will be an important document in your future. It's where you bring together everything relevant to your career, a repository where you keep and update all your career information.

Later in Chapter Seven, you'll build your resumé based on the information in this report.

You won't use all this material in your resumé. But each time you prepare to send your resumé to a prospective employer, this document will be there for you to refer to. You'll be able to pick and choose information specific to the job you're applying for.

I want to emphasize that this person of interest report will become your core document, your go-to place for information. As you'll see in Chapter Seven, your resumé will be customized and change each time you apply for a position. However, the person of interest report will be your constant source of information, only changing when you update it with new information.

I recommend you review it twice a year and update when you have new information.

Every time you update the document, note the date. Then, when you're ready to launch your second career, you know you'll have the most up-to-date information.

You've written many reports by this stage of your career. No doubt you're quite capable of writing a police report about a person of interest. However, I'm going to suggest a format for this particular report so that you don't miss anything important.

First, let's look at how you might approach your person of interest report.

Be thorough. This will be the basis for your resumé. So be sure to include everything that's important. Write in a way that is comfortable for you. Use bullets and lists if that makes the document clearer for you.

Be honest with yourself when you write this report. Imagine that you're going to be cross-examined in court about it. Make it completely accurate, just as you would in preparing a report for court.

Draw the contents of the report from the information you put in your career blocks (Chapter Three) and the lists you created from your analysis (Chapter Four).

Break the report into sections. Below, I've put in some section titles. I'd suggest you use them and fill in the information from your unique police career.

Timeline: List all your main assignments and the dates they started and finished. Include the dates you worked at all jobs and the date you started at your police agency.

For instance: Police academy training from ___ to ___. Patrol Division assignment and where from ___ to ___. Include specialty squads, promotions and significant special projects.

Your foundation: Use the information from Block A to write about your foundation. Give examples of your academic and training accomplishments.

For example, when writing about your pre-police education and experience, note any special recognition.

Comment about your reputation as you believe it to be.

Your skills: In Chapter Four, you analyzed your police career and listed all your skills. Now include them in this report. From now on, when you learn a new skill, add it to this document.

Your top three strengths: Give two examples of when you demonstrated each of your strengths. Add any lesser strengths.

Your three weaknesses: Give two examples of times when you demonstrated each weakness.

Later, in Chapter Six, we'll discuss where you might want to improve your skills package. You'll find it helpful to have identified these key weaknesses.

Certifications and Professional Designations: List any such qualifications you have. For example, you may be a Certified Fraud Examiner or an accident reconstruction expert. You may hold a specialized training designation.

Include all your certifications and professional designations, even those not related to your police career. Collect them all in your report so you can use them later.

Memberships: List memberships in any organizations you belong to, even if not related to your professional life.

Your contacts and network: This goes hand in hand with your memberships. However, your contacts and network include all the informal connections you have. Think about who you know. (Have a look at the networking books on my website at secondcareersforstreetcops.com. There are good suggestions in each of them.)

Volunteer activities: Write about any volunteer work you do. This could include coaching a sports team, helping out with work at a religious organization, being a member of a Board of Directors for a volunteer agency, etc.

What you would like to do for a second career: In Chapter Two, I asked you to start thinking about what kind of work you'd like to do. Now that you've done some analysis, think hard about what you want for a second career.

You may have a long time to go in your police career so perhaps there's lots of time to prepare. On the other hand, you may be ready to go now. The timing of your move will determine the urgency of your choice.

Based on what you know about yourself right now, list three possible second careers that appeal to you. Describe each of the three second careers in detail.

As you examine each possible career move, knowing the specifics will help you decide which to choose.

What have you always wanted to do? In Chapter Two, you considered your dream job. Maybe you included it in the last item. However, those three choices were probably driven a lot by practical realities. That's fine, and it certainly is important to think realistically about what you might consider for a second career. There are many important real-life considerations that affect the choices you made for your three likely possibilities.

But set the practicalities aside, and think again about the one thing you've always wanted to do for a career.

Perhaps the option of still doing it no longer exists… But maybe it's still out there for you.

Give yourself the opportunity to at least think freely about it. Write about your dream job. If it doesn't seem possible now, it may in the future.

When will you be ready to move to a second career? Maybe you're ready now. If so, work your way through this book and go for it. However, you may be looking ahead any number of years.

It's helpful to have a time period in mind because of the many issues affecting such a move. You may have financial goals to meet first or police career goals or educational goals that will help you launch a second career.

Write the date you plan to launch your second career. Even if it seems far off, get a date down in your report. You can always change it.

> Tip #5: Be ready. Opportunities have a surprising way of happening when you least expect them. Keep the information in this document up to date.

Part of being ready is keeping this person of interest document up to date so you can draw on your most current career information when opportunity knocks on your door.

Where do you want to live during your second career? Name three places. Give yourself the opportunity to think freely about this. Maybe you'll be happy right where you live now. But perhaps a part of you has always wanted to move to that special place.

Are you willing to go where the work takes you? That's something to think about when considering your second career.

List the three places you would like to live most.

The money: At some point you'll need to decide how much you want to be paid and how much money you need. You should give this consideration in whatever way works for you. Consider seeking the advice of a financial advisor.

Courtesy of JohnPWeiss.com

Now that you have focused on all your skills, think about six attributes that you consider are applicable to you. For example: decisive, flexible, ethical, team player, committed, focused, etc.

These are broad descriptors of your character and approach to work. They will help you focus on your most descriptive attributes when you're building your resumé.

Update: Each time you update this report, put the date in at the end. You'll find this very helpful in staying clear about when you added new information.

Now you have your core document completed. After all the work you have put into this, do yourself a big favor and make a back-up copy. You wouldn't want to do this again.

Often in investigations, there comes a time when we sit back and ask ourselves what we've missed. That's next, in Chapter Six.

CHAPTER 6

Fill the Gaps in Your Investigation. What's Missing in your Skills Package?

You have your person of interest document completed. Now let's look at what you can do to strengthen that document.

This chapter is about gaps in your qualifications or experience. Don't be concerned, everyone has something missing from their skills package. However, not everyone takes the time to figure out what's missing and fill in those gaps.

> Tip #6: You need a solid foundation to build your portfolio on. Think about what's missing.

Your strengths and weaknesses: In Chapter Four you identified your strengths and weaknesses. Then, in Chapter Five, you thought about some examples of each.

Obviously your strengths are not the problem. They're what you do well and rely on to get through each day.

But it's time to look your weaknesses in the eye and figure out what to do about them. Look for easy fixes here though. Don't drive yourself crazy fixing a perceived weakness that isn't going to change your job future. Instead, go back to your strengths and build on what you are good at. Turn your good strengths into excellent strengths, attributes that you can use to really make a difference in finding a second career.

You listed your three top weaknesses and noted some examples of each. If you were able to do that, you're probably pretty clear about what they are. Now it's just a matter of figuring out what to do with them.

Remember, we've all got weaknesses. You're not alone here. Lots of people have had great careers in spite of their weaknesses.

Think about the ones you've identified and how they will impact your opportunity to move on to a second career. Fix them now and improve your portfolio by doing so. For instance, if you identified report writing as a weakness, improve your report writing skills by seeking some training through your police agency. If speaking to groups is a problem, take some training in presentation skills.

I mentioned earlier that the work you do in relation to this book is all about YOUR career. You don't need to share it with anyone. So you're the only one who knows what you've identified as your key weaknesses. If there aren't some easy ways to fix them, consider some professional career counseling.

Gaps in your qualifications: What were your top three choices for a second career? Compare your skills package with those three jobs and ask yourself whether or not you're qualified. List some qualifications here you'd like to have to up your chance of success.

Specialized training: Perhaps some training is required for the second career of your choice. Maybe you need some specialized training or certification.

Here's an example. You've decided you want to become a private investigator as a second career. I mention the PI example because I'm a big believer in building on what you know, and street cops know how to investigate.

The PI business is heavily regulated. That's not necessarily a bad thing. However, if this is a second career that interests you, it will be important to understand what those regulations are. How do they affect your opportunity to get a PI license? Do you feel all right working within those regulations?

Your experience as a police officer is usually a great step toward qualifying for a PI license. But, in some places your police experience will only be accepted for a certain period of time. After that you may need to qualify by taking specialized PI training.

For example, in British Columbia a former police officer can acquire a PI license without further training within five years of leaving a police agency. You'd need to research those time limitations in your jurisdiction and apply for a license before the time period expires.

You could get the specialized training or professional designation before you leave your police career to increase your chances of employment as a PI. For example, you might want to train to become a Certified Fraud Examiner. An assignment to the fraud or commercial crime section in your police agency would certainly help toward acquiring that kind of knowledge.

There are other certifications relative to PI work that you might want to pursue. Perhaps you'd like to be a traffic accident reconstruction specialist for your second career. Obviously if you spend some time in your police career working at this specialty, you'll be better equipped to carry it on into a second career.

What kind of investigating would you like to do? Private investigators do a lot of surveillance. I enjoyed doing surveillance when I was around forty years old. I'm not sure I'd like doing surveillance at age fifty or sixty. However, private investigators do other things too, such as background checks, pre-employment investigations, insurance fraud investigations, and locating missing persons. Match your skills even further with the type of PI work you are interested in.

Remember Kevin McQuiggin, the thirty-year cop who became a professional pilot? He filled in the gaps in his qualifications. He had a private pilot's license and knew he wanted to fly jet aircraft some day. So he figured out what he needed to do in order to qualify to fly the larger planes. Then, he filled in the gaps by getting further pilot certification.

Plan your police career moves: Be strategic as you look ahead to a second career. Specialize in your future second career before you even leave your police agency, if you have that opportunity. You might improve your preparation considerably by doing so.

For example, conducting polygraph interviews is very specialized. There are opportunities to work in this field after policing, but you would be in a much better position to do so if you'd received the training and experience during your policing career.

Work toward matching your skills with the future job you have in mind. Fill in the gaps. Get the training you need for your second career while you're still in your first career.

Dave Jones is president of the Private Investigators' Association of British Columbia. As he reflected on his police career, Dave realized he would have benefited from more specific training. He said: "If I had looked ahead to becoming a private investigator, I could have used more training, such as statement analysis or advanced interviewing techniques. Those are useful in other careers too, such as the human resources field."

Network: Who has a better network than street cops? We all know someone who knows someone. But there seems to be some kind of stigma to the word "networking."

Look, unless you're a hermit, you come in contact with a lot of people. Some of them may be connected to future careers that you're interested in. There's nothing wrong or devious about remembering who they are and asking them a question or for some advice.

Many people enjoy talking about their work life and are pleased to offer suggestions. That's all we're talking about here, not some sinister plot to take unfair advantage of anyone. Besides, street cops are quick to ask fellow street cops for a recommendation about where to buy, travel, or look for advice. Expand that network beyond your street cop contacts. Fill in your networking gaps, particularly in career fields you're interested in.

Dave Jones was nearing the end of his police career and was assigned to the business district in downtown Vancouver. He made many contacts in the business community while carrying out his police duties. As a result, Dave had a job offer to leave policing and become a security consultant to the Downtown Vancouver Business Improvement Association.

This is networking at its best. You meet a lot of people in policing. Good things can happen as a result. Dave went on to have a successful second career as a security consultant and private investigator.

I asked Jack Ewatski, the former Winnipeg police chief, if he had any advice to pass on to today's police officers about finding a second career. He had this to say: "First, they should look for opportunities on the job. Take advantage of training opportunities during your police career. And second, make good connections. Think about the people you meet on courses from other jurisdictions. Make connections with them and keep those connections. Networking is so easy in policing."

Create a Professional online presence: Understand that you can do a lot online to find a second career. There are some good resources on my website about creating your online presence. LinkedIn is a good place to start. Set up your profile on LinkedIn and start networking professionally. It's free and gives you lots of possibilities to work with. I haven't found any other site that is as focused on career and employment issues.

I use LinkedIn to organize my network and suggest you do the same. It's easy and efficient.

You really need to do this if you're looking ahead to future employment. Within LinkedIn, there are many job-hunting groups set up for you to join or follow to keep up with the latest information about careers and career changing.

Big hint here: Take the time to understand how LinkedIn works so you can get maximum benefit out of it. There are lots of free workshops around. Check your library. It may have some coming up. LinkedIn also runs its own online, free tutorials.

Organizations related to your second career choices: In Chapter Five, you listed the organizations that you had memberships in. Now look ahead and do some research into organizations related to your second career choice. Do the organizations you're a member of relate to your second career choices? If not, that might be a gap you want to fill. You could find groups on LinkedIn related to the organizations.

Would you be able to join such an organization before you start your second career? There are excellent opportunities to meet those already working in the field through conferences, seminars, or social gatherings. You can make a lot of contacts and discover much about your future second career in this way.

For example, if you're planning to enter the private security industry as a second career you could consider a membership in ASIS International, (formerly the American Society for Industrial Security). This is a large, well-known, global organization for security professionals.

ASIS International provides training and professional designations in several security areas. ASIS International holds conferences at various places throughout the world and there are many opportunities to learn about the security business through their programs.

Other industries provide similar opportunities. It would be to your benefit to spend some time researching organizations in your particular field of interest. Take these very early steps of transitioning to your second career.

Certifications and Professional Designations: Keep these in mind. If you don't have them, you might need to get them. Do it before you leave your police career if possible.

As you build your portfolio for a second career, consider how the credentials available from an organization related to your second career choice, such as ASIS International, could enhance your suitability for a future employer. You'd be building on your police career foundation and filling in the missing gaps in your portfolio at the same time.

Finish your education: How you do this will really depend on the education you have now. You may have a good enough educational background for your second career. In that case, you'd probably be better off finding the specialized training required to improve your chances for success.

You may have started post secondary schooling and never finished your diploma or degree program. Take the opportunity to do that while you're still in your policing career, if it will help you move to a second career.

Shift work and unusual hours can make this difficult. However, there are many credible online post-secondary programs available now. It isn't necessary to attend classroom lectures at a specific time each week to earn a degree.

Get published: This is a great way to build your portfolio. There are many publications related to policing and law enforcement that you could write an article for. This is the icing on the cake for someone putting together a resumé based on a police career. Including the titles of your published material in your resumé gives a potential employer some information about you.

When I review a resumé and see a reference to published material, I'm always interested in reading what that person has written. Take advantage of this opportunity while you're still an active police officer.

Filling in these gaps becomes part of your ops plan, which you'll design later. Once you've identified the gaps you want to work on, it just becomes a matter of doing it as you get closer to your second career. Filling in the gaps improves your person of interest portfolio document by increasing your qualifications and getting you better prepared to move on.

Before you start looking for a second career though, it's best to have a resumé ready to go. That's what the next chapter is all about.

CHAPTER 7

Record of Investigation. Your Resumé

Courtesy of JohnPWeiss.com

You've created your Person of Interest document (Chapter 5) and looked at where the gaps in your portfolio are (Chapter 6). This chapter is about how you approach putting a resumé together.

> Tip #7: Have a resumé ready to go.

I reviewed about 2000 resumés when I was hiring investigators at WorkSafeBC. I never saw two that were in the same format. Each one was different in some way. There was no perfect format and no perfect length of a resumé.

Those applying for investigator jobs used every creative way imaginable to draw attention to their resumés. Some submitted theirs on brightly colored paper; some came in plastic or paper folders. Others sent along attachments about investigations they had conducted. Some submitted overly brief resumés with almost no information. Still others submitted resumés that were too long at six or eight pages.

I was looking for high quality talent that matched the skills needed for the position advertised. When I found that, it was usually in a fairly simple resumé with no glitz but lots of depth in investigative experience.

There were some resumés that didn't stand a chance. Believe it or not, some people submitted resumés for the wrong job! I received resumés for positions not even related to the investigator jobs I was advertising. Applicants apparently didn't take the time to update their resumés or customize them to the investigator position that was posted.

Imagine how unappealing it is to receive a resumé for the last job the person applied for instead of the position you're trying to fill!

Customize to the job posting: When you're submitting a resumé, carefully review the job requirements and match your skills to those listed in the job posting. This means customizing your resumé to the job you're applying for.

Details, details: In Chapter Five you created your Person of Interest document. That's your repository of skills, talents, strengths, and credentials. Use that document as you customize your resumé to a particular job. <u>Pay very close attention to the specific details of the job posting. Then tailor your resumé to those details.</u>

Apply if you're close: Those job posting details may note that experience in a particular field may be sufficient if an applicant lacks formal credentials. For instance, some jobs ask for a university degree but will accept some types of experience in its place. You may not have a degree but could have had lots of training and experience. If you think you meet that type of qualification, apply anyway. If your qualifications move you close to what the posting is asking for, you might get an interview.

Some job postings scare potential applicants away. Don't just give up. As a street cop you've had to be assertive. Use that assertiveness to go for it if you think you have a chance.

Make it easy for them: Some organizations now ask that an applicant's resumé be submitted electronically. The instructions are usually pretty simple. However, they typically ask for a valid file format or software to be used when uploading your resumé. Do follow their instructions and submit in the requested format.

Don't make it difficult for the person reviewing your electronic submission to open it. The harder the reviewer has to work at opening the document, the less likely it is that your resumé will get the attention you want it to have. Make it easy for them.

> Tip #8: Protect your integrity and the integrity of your police agency.

Law & Policy: Keep secret what is supposed to be secret. Don't breach the law or the confidentiality policy of your police agency. Street cops have the most amazing experiences and access to a lot of confidential information. It's important to remember that what's secret has to stay secret.

It's one thing to display your skills and talent in your resumé but quite another to breach privacy laws or the policy of your organization by composing a tell-all resumé.

I had very sensitive assignments that didn't go in my resumé. However, some of the skills I learned during those assignments quite legitimately ended up in my skills package.

Keep that in mind as you compose your resumé. Stick to the skills and experience you offer and stay within the limits of law and policy. You maintain your own integrity by doing so and respect the policies of your police agency at the same time.

You may end up sending your resumé to a large number of potential employers and there will be things you know that are not for wide dissemination. A good employer should respect your understanding of the need for confidentiality.

Integrity is expected of a street cop. It's a strength you'll be expected to have. I posted a job for an investigator position a few years ago and received a number of applications. The most promising ones made my shortlist, and I was getting ready to ask one of the applicants in for an interview when, to my surprise, he phoned me:"I'm right in the middle of a big investigation and I just can't walk away from it. If I'm your successful candidate, I'm going to have to withdraw my application for now."

His sense of integrity and commitment impressed me. Eventually he was hired.

> Tip #9: Update your resumé at least twice a year. Note the date when you do it.

Keep your resumé current: This just makes life easier for you and ensures you don't forget to include something important. There are a couple of surprise scenarios that can cause you to scramble to update your resumé in a big hurry. Then you have the additional problem of remembering things when you're under time pressure. Chances are you'll miss something.

The first surprise is when you spot a job you're interested in but don't have an updated resumé ready to go. That puts you in scramble mode as you try to catch up in a hurry to meet the posting deadline.

For example, near the end of my police career, I was keeping my eye open for second career opportunities. All of a sudden, there it was: WorkSafeBC advertised for a position in their Investigations Division. At the time, I was still in a very busy job at the Vancouver

Police Department. I didn't have time to drop everything and create a resumé. Luckily, I had one ready to go and with a few minor adjustments, submitted it by the posting deadline. Soon after, I jumped to my new job. (I would have liked a little more vacation time between careers but didn't want to turn down a great opportunity.)

Another surprise is when someone contacts you because they're interested in hiring you. You may have come to their attention as a potential employee for any number of reasons. The phone rings, and suddenly you're considering a career move.

"Send me your resumé" becomes a panic situation rather than a good opportunity.

You can see how helpful it will be in both these cases to have a resumé up to date so that, with a few changes, you can respond easily. It's way more problematic and stressful interrupting your busy life to spend a lot of unplanned time hastily putting together a resumé.

So be ready.

Resumé format: The style and format of your resumé is a very personal choice. Before designing your own, I'd suggest you look at how the experts do it.

There are many good resumé resources available for you to examine. Your public library or the careers/business section of a book store should have lots. The resumé books usually have plenty of sample formats to choose from. Examine some of the excellent resumé books listed on my website to see what format works for you. There are also resumé preparation software packages available for purchase at computer stores or online.

An internet search results in an overwhelming response of resumé writing resources. This may be one of those cases where a resumé writing book in your hand is a lot simpler than trying to sift through the many listed in your internet search. Start with your free public library. Before you compose your resumé, I'd suggest having a look at a couple of these. Examine their sample resumés to find a format that suits you.

I found *Knock 'em Dead Resumes* by Martin Yate to be one of the best around. It's right up to date and very thorough with lots of examples.

Two other books about resumé preparation that I particularly liked were *The Career Change Resumé* by Kim Isaacs and Karen Hofferber, and *Best Canadian Resumés* by Sharon Graham. They're especially good because both books have an example of a resumé prepared by a police officer. You'd probably find them useful as you consider the format of your resumé.

A professional resumé writer: You could hire a professional resumé writer to put together the best possible resumé. Some of us need a professional to produce a really polished document. The service wouldn't be free, but you might end up with a much better resumé.

There might be problems, or negative aspects, to your police career that need to be stated delicately. Street cops, like everyone else, have histories. And they're not always good. If that is your situation, you might want to hire a professional resumé writer to help you put together the best resumé presentation possible.

Shop around, as you would when purchasing any service. It's easy to hire a professional resumé writer from many parts of the world simply by making contact on the internet.

Keep cultural and spelling differences in mind. It won't help to submit a well polished resumé that contains odd spellings or reflects cultural differences. That could immediately identify you as a bad fit for the job.

Resumé formats and presentation methods evolve and change like a lot of other things in our world. A professional resumé writer should be aware of the latest styles and methods of submitting a resumé.

Some resumé writers have a professional designation, such as the Certified Professional Resumé Writer (CPRW) or the Nationally Certified Resumé Writer (NCRW). Others have a long history of success in the resumé writing business. Look for these professional assets when selecting who will prepare this important document for you.

Check references and ask to see some of the work they've done. It would be helpful if they had some knowledge of police work and the second career you're interested in. There's an excellent article called *How to Select a Resume Writer* by freelance journalist Lisa Vaas on The Ladders website. If you think you're going to do this, I'd strongly recommend you read the article first.

> Tip #10: Make a back-up copy of your resumé. You'll never remember everything that's in it if your computer crashes and you lose the information.

CHAPTER **8**

Every Investigation Needs an Operational Plan. Design Yours

"I'm not sure you understand what I mean by career goals."

Cartoon by Mark Anderson

Let's review how far you've come in your second career investigation project:

- In Chapter One, you considered the value of your police career. Like any investigation, you thought about whether it was worth doing.

- You started your investigation in Chapter Two by assessing the situation. You gave more thought to a second career.

- In Chapter Three, you collected all your police career facts in one place.

- Continuing your investigation in Chapter Four, you did an analysis of your strengths and weaknesses.

- In Chapter Five, you wrote your Person of Interest report. You brought all your experience and skills together in one document.

- Chapter Six was where you examined what's missing in your portfolio. You considered what you can do to fill in the gaps, what skills needed developing, or what experiences you would like to have.

- Chapter Seven gave you some information about planning a resumé.

Congratulations. Give yourself a pat on the back for all your hard work.

Chapter Eight is where you design your operational plan and set some goals for yourself. The shape this plan takes depends a lot on how soon you'll be ready to launch your second career.

If you've only got a short time to go before leaving policing or if you've already left, you're probably ready to start your second career search now.

On the other hand, if you're in mid-career and have ten or fifteen years to go, you'll want to design a longer term plan that can be revised as time passes.

We're going to use the longer term plan to show you some good ideas to keep building your portfolio and plan ahead. If you're ready to jump to a second career now, skip the parts you don't have time for and go back to them later after you're settled in your new career.

Keep in mind that you're not locked into any of this. It's YOUR plan to update and change any time you wish. It's yours. You own it.

Your Second Career Plan

1: Pick a date when you want to start your second career. A self-imposed deadline will help with your planning. Call it Start Second Career Date and put it in your Ops Plan document. Write it in here for easy reference.

_____

_____

_____

_____

_____

2: Choose your second career. If you're not sure or it's just too far off, pick three possibilities. Name your choice(s) here.

_____

_____

_____

_____

_____

_____

3: Keep filling in those gaps you identified in Chapter Six. Go back and review your notes. What did you identify that could help you improve your career portfolio? Choose the most important ones and insert them into this plan.

Go back to Chapter Six from time to time to see what's still missing. Identify new gaps. Consider some of the career enhancing suggestions in Chapter Five.

Name two career enhancing strategies you would like to work on here. For example, joining an organization, attending a conference, or taking a course.

_____

_____

_____

_____

_____

_____

_____

4: Identify the new skills you have learned as time passes. Update your Person of Interest document and resumé.

5: Keep scanning the workplace horizon for **new career possibilities** and job trends. Use the job trend resources on my website.

6: Consider getting help, particularly if you aren't clear about some aspect of planning for your second career.

You may want to hire a career coach, a professional resumé writer, a financial advisor, or other professionals.

I don't think everyone needs the help of professionals, but there are times when someone with special insight can help you move forward. They can be a great help, especially if you find one you can connect with.

7: Stay healthy and fit to the best of your ability. I found, as I got older, that work takes a greater toll on the body and mind. It can be stimulating and a very positive force in your life. But, there is no denying that the stress and strain of work is often harder to handle at fifty or sixty than when you're thirty. Staying fit gave me the stamina to take on a very demanding second career. There's no guarantee you'll be able to keep on working as you get older. You can't count on having the good health to do so, but staying as healthy and fit as possible will surely help.

8: Be the best street cop you can be. Remember Tip #2 in Chapter Two about the value of your reputation? Work hard at your police career. Stay interested. Take advantage of training opportunities. Look for assignments that would be good preparation for your second career. Build that reputation.

9: Review your ops plan once a year. Change and update it as necessary. Write a date for your first review in your calendar. Each time you review it, note the date.

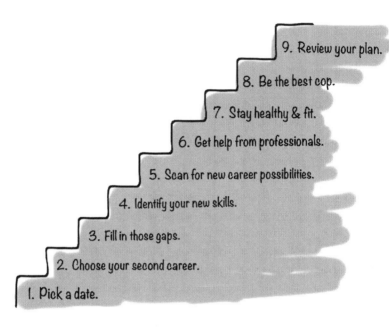

Diagram by Brad Hill

Tip #11: Pick a hero. Find someone you admire who has gone on to a successful second career. Discover how they did it and make their strategies work for you.

CHAPTER 9

Follow-up. Looking Ahead

Cartoon by Brad Hill

You've done your analysis, organized your profile, written a resumé, and developed an operational plan. I hope you feel a sense of accomplishment and optimism after all your hard work.

However, the work is not over. In fact, it never ends. But in a good way. The tedious part is behind you. You can realistically look to the future now and build on your ops plan. Start watching for all the great opportunities out there knowing that you're ready to launch whenever the job for you comes along.

This chapter is about you looking ahead to a second career, keeping informed about employment trends and opportunities that interest you.

Who knows what the job future holds? There's as much disagreement on this as on other topics. Besides, who has the crystal ball that can say with certainty where the jobs will be? And who can you trust enough to believe they got it right?

Street cops usually have a healthy streak of cynicism anyway. They don't believe a lot of what they hear. Go with that. Trust your instincts. Follow your operational plan.

Keep an interest in job trends and new career possibilities but focus on the second career choices you put in your ops plan.

Stay up to date on the employment areas of your choice. Watch the trends in those jobs closely. You'll want to know if job opportunities are trending upward or downward in the second career you're planning for. As time goes by, you may decide one is better than the others. That could help focus your plan as far as training, upgrading skills, or network contacts are concerned.

Look for media articles, books, industry organizations, conferences, seminars, and educational opportunities.

There's lots of information available, but there's not one magic source that has it all. Look for groups on LinkedIn that relate to your second career choices. For example, there are groups for security, investigations, careers, police, and many more.

Keep at it by staying alert to what's developing in the jobs you're interested in.

Credible media sources can be very helpful. Sifting through government websites can be like searching a suspect for drugs. You may eventually find what you're looking for but the process can be long and unpleasant. Often it's more helpful to use reliable media sources. Confirm the information later.

Government websites are not all bad though. Here are some of the better ones that I found.

The U.S. Department of Labor - Bureau of Labor Statistics website has projections for the fastest growing occupations through 2022. It also lists occupations with the most job growth. Look for the summary of employment projections in the same section.

In England and Wales, the **National Association of Police Officers (NARPO)** has some employment postings on its website. The Blue Line Jobs website is also a good place to look. Its subtitle is The Police & Criminal Justice Community Job Site. There is good information available at the Police into Private Sector (PIPS) website.

The government website of Human Resources and Skills Development Canada has a section called the Canadian Occupational Projection System. The acronym is COPS. (I'm not kidding.) COPS has a search tool that projects labor demand for 140 occupations in Canada through 2020.

Get your hands on a copy of the *MacLean's Magazine 2015 Guide to Jobs in Canada.* It's an excellent examination and summary of where the best opportunities are and will be in the future.

The **Australian government website** has a very user-friendly Job Outlook section. There are job description overviews and job prospects projected to 2017.

Likewise, the **New Zealand government** has a medium – long term employment outlook on its website, projecting industry needs and occupations through 2021. Go to Ministry of Business, Innovation and Employment, Research Centre, Labor Market Information, Forecasting.

There are many great resources mentioned on my website. Make good use of them. Pick a few and start from there. Resist the shotgun approach of looking at so many sites, books and articles that you come away overwhelmed and bewildered.

While I had a long police career followed by a successful second career, I'm not a career management or human resources expert. I believe the ops plan you have developed will help you follow a similar path. Now, I want to leave you with some direction about where to go from here. Consider what the following people have to say.

These four resources are among the best there are to help you plan for a second career. These people have the professional credentials to help you learn more. Their websites have lots of free information that you will find helpful. They also have free newsletters, blogs, and postings that will help keep you up to date on career and employment issues.

Four top sites where you can learn more:

1. Nancy Collamer is a career coach, speaker, and author of *Second-Act Careers.* Her website is MyLifestyleCareer.com. Both her site and her book are very good for our purposes because they focus on issues relative to second careers. This is a resource with lots of useful information. For example, there's an article on her site called *Want To Research A Retirement Career?*

2. Martin Yate has been in the career management business for thirty-five years. Knock Em Dead.com is his website and the name he gives to his books. He's really someone to listen to when considering a career move. His website includes topics such as resumé writing, coaching, books and career advice. Take a look at the article he has posted on his site about *Savvy Strategies For Overcoming Unspoken Age-Bias.*

3. The Five O'clock Club – Join the club and get some good career advice. I've looked at their resources and they're very good. Career coaching, self-help, and lending a hand to others with their careers, is all part of what they do. The site is at fiveoclockclub.com

4. Richard N. Bolles comes out every year with a new version of his book *What Color Is Your Parachute? - A Practical Manual for Job-Hunters & Career Changers.* His companion website is JobHuntersBible.com. There's a

great deal of career information here and you're sure to find it useful when considering a career move.

As you explore these and the other resources at the back of this book, you'll discover new ideas that work for you. Let me know about them so I can let other street cops know through my blog.

I keep an updated list of resources and organizations on my website at www.secondcareersforstreetcops.com. My blog is all about second careers for street cops and retired cops. I'll be adding new material and resources to the site as it becomes available. It's there to help you. You can also follow me on Twitter @copsecondcareer where I post second career updates.

As you go through your police career, remember to look ahead and always have your plan for a second career in mind. Think strategically about the positions you take in your police agency and the training opportunities that come your way. Will they help you build a better foundation for your second career?

Persevere. Look ahead.

Here's my last tip.

Tip #12: Keep at it. Careers and work life have their ups and downs. Don't give up on your dream of a second career if that's what you want after your police career. Lots of street cops have done it. You can too. Good luck. Best wishes.

CHAPTER **10**

More Second Career Stories. From Street Cop to ...

Corporate Investigator: Ramon Garcia was an FBI agent for twenty-five years. Like all of us who have had a long career in law enforcement, he had a large, informal network of contacts. Through a friend of a friend in his network, Ramon became aware of a second career opportunity. He had retired from the FBI when this opportunity came along and decided to take up a second career, conducting internal investigations for a large corporation.

He had this to say for those looking ahead to a second career: "Look around and see what training and assignment opportunities interest you within your organization before you leave policing. Try to match those up with your future plans. When you decide on a second career, get into something you really want to do. A lot of police officers continue on as investigators but not everyone wants to do that after a police career. There are lots of other things to work at."

Ramon remembers he was very interested in working in the hotel business after he left the FBI. That didn't happen. Looking back, he feels he would have benefited by networking more in the hotel industry so he could have taken advantage of employment opportunities that might have come up.

Think about your future. Is there an industry or business sector that you're particularly interested in for a second career? Try to learn more about it now while you have time to plan. Establish some contacts in the business or take some training that will help you transition to the job you're interested in. Is there an association you could join associated to the business? How about a conference? They're a great way to learn about an industry or business.

Ramon stayed with his second career for four and a half years. Then he decided to leave that position and take a volunteer opportunity with the American Red Cross. He approaches his volunteer duties with the same degree of enthusiasm and initiative he used in his first two careers. He has an opportunity to use the skills he learned in law enforcement to deal with people in crisis situations. Recently, he was called out to assist with an emergency situation after a serious fire in an apartment building. He feels his leadership and organizational skills will continue to be put to good use as he learns more about carrying out his volunteer duties.

Like most of us who have left law enforcement, there are parts of the job Ramon misses. He reflected on his FBI career and remembered how much he enjoyed being part of a large organization with its structure and many contacts. Ramon loved being an FBI agent and still feels the FBI is one of the greatest organizations in the world. Being part of the American Red Cross fills that void. Even though its work is not law enforcement, he enjoys the camaraderie that comes with doing a difficult and meaningful job.

Private Investigator: I met Tom Dolo for the first time in the mid-1980's when we worked together in the Vancouver Police Department (VPD) Strike Force. We were part of a surveillance squad that worked on very active, high profile criminal investigations. He's an excellent investigator, a smart and experienced guy who now has almost forty years of experience. Today, he's the owner of one of the largest private investigations firms in British Columbia, Dolo Investigations.

Tom is a self-described Type A personality, someone that likes to be on the go a lot and enjoys the excitement of a good investigation.

After seventeen years of police service with two organizations, the VPD and the Royal Canadian Mounted Police, he decided to put his high energy, skills, and experience to work in the corporate sector. Tom set out to learn about the world of private investigations.

It took a lot of work to build his business. For the first few years, he worked six days a week to get the company up and running – and on a secure footing.

Tom's police career experience gave him the skills and knowledge he needed to adapt to corporate investigations. As part of his PI career, he has been the president of the Private Investigators' Association of BC and served in other PIABC office positions. Tom has now had the benefit of a great deal of experience in both the public sector police environment and the private sector. He has some tough-love advice for police officers who want to move into private investigations:

"Your police skills are valuable. But police experience doesn't give you a free ride in the PI world. Even though you've had a badge, you have to prove yourself. There are high expectations if you go to work for a PI firm. The young PIs are willing to work long and hard so be prepared to keep up with them. Get rid of any sense of entitlement. The badge will open doors but you'll have to prove yourself. Be aggressive."

And if you plan to start your own private investigations firm, Tom had this to say: "You can make a good living at PI work. Be prepared to work hard. It's as much about the business as it is about investigating. You have to do the preparation to set up a business. Get some good financial advice, including tax advice. Go to a proper tax advisor. Have enough cash on hand to get started. You'll need cash reserves if you're expanding or hiring. Advertise on social media such as Facebook, Twitter, and LinkedIn. Be prepared to learn some of this the hard way."

Deputy Police Commissioner and Police Studies instructor: Jack Ewatski was a police officer in the Winnipeg Police Service for thirty-four years. He was the Chief of Police for his last nine years. During his time as Chief he was president of the Canadian Association of Chiefs of Police.

When Jack left the WPS, he took some time to decompress from all those years of policing and think about what he wanted to do next. He said: "I knew I was going to do something but I took some time to think about it. I wasn't going to just put my feet up. I thought about what I would really like to do."

Jack became a security consultant in the private sector for awhile. Then an interesting opportunity presented itself. He became a Deputy Police Commissioner of the Trinidad and Tobago Police Service. He was able to call on his long experience in policing to take on these new challenges in another country. After two years in that position he returned to Canada and again thought about what he'd like to do.

Jack had always enjoyed the training aspect of policing and spent three and a half years in the Training Section of the Winnipeg Police. He knew he enjoyed teaching and presenting ideas in a classroom setting. Another opportunity presented itself. Assiniboine Community College in Brandon, Manitoba was looking for an instructor in its Police Studies program. Jack was hired and today enjoys teaching in the Integrated Police Studies program.

Realtor: Neil Thompson was a police officer for twenty-seven years. By the time he got to the end of his police career, he had had quite enough of working in the criminal justice system.

Neil wanted to try something different, so he became a realtor. It didn't happen overnight. He took about a year after he left policing to consider what he wanted to do for a second career. A good friend of his was a realtor and the more Neil learned about it, the more he thought it would work for him.

After getting certified as a licensed realtor, he was up and running and into the business world of real estate sales. Seventeen years later, he's still at his successful second career with million dollar listings.

Neil found that his police experience was good preparation for the skills he uses as a realtor. Communication and mediation skills, dealing with people in stressful situations, all are useful in his work.

"Buying a home can be one of the most stressful things a person does," Neil said. "The things I learned as a police officer really help in dealing with people in those situations."

Didn't think your police experience was valuable in the business world? Think again.

Recommended Reading

I reviewed a lot of books, web sites, and articles during this book project. Those listed here are some that I found particularly useful. You'll find lots more on my website at secondcareersforstreetcops.com.

There aren't any duds in this group. If I didn't think a particular reference would be helpful to you, I didn't use it. You just need to find which ones apply to your situation.

Some of us aren't book readers and get information in other ways. If that's you, I've noted some magazine articles and links on my website that are quicker information hits.

The Encore Career Handbook – How To Make A Living And A Difference In The Second Half Of Life by Marci Alboher (2013). This is the book for those who want to make the world a better place and get paid for doing it. More than that though, there are good chapters on self-assessment, networking, and trying out new careers. Also, check out the website Encore.org.

Second-Act Careers by Nancy Collamer (2013). This is a very good book by a well-known speaker and author. The book is a good combination of advice and self-assessment. She has ten excellent key questions for you to work through to guide yourself forward. Most are simple questions but they'll make you think about what is going to work for you.

What Color is Your Parachute? A Practical Manual for Job-Hunters & Career-Changers by Richard N. Bolles (2014). This is a big book, big as in important for career-changers and second career seekers. If you want to dig deep and really look at a lot of aspects of career questions, this is a good book for you.

Encore – Finding Work That Matters in the Second Half of Life by Marc Freedman (2008). Another good book about finding meaning in the second half of life. It's very sincere, with good examples of those that have done it.

Your Next Career. Do What You've Always Wanted to Do by Gail Geary (2010). She has some important comments about staying current with employment trends. She also addresses some of the reasons people stay in careers they don't like and then asks the reader to name their own fears about changing careers. She's very thorough and takes the reader through the whole range of career changing. There's a good chapter on working in the post-retirement years.

The Power of Reputation by Chris Komisarjevsky (2012). Our reputation is so personal. Few of us have much of a strategy for keeping it intact beyond doing our best and hoping all goes well. This book is a behind-the-scenes look at how to understand and manage your reputation. It's a good way to learn more about this important feature of your second career portfolio. And it becomes an even more important read if you think your reputation is a problem for you. Published by AMACOM, a division of American Management Association. (www.amacombooks.org)

Transitions by Michael V. Maddaloni (2002). This is a guide on moving from law enforcement or the military into a second career and a good book to get you started. It's not very big at 102 pages but hits on some of the main things to consider in planning for a second career. The author is a former Secret Service Agent.

Second Acts – Creating the Life You Really Want, Building the Career You Truly Desire by Stephen M. Pollan and Mark Levine (2003). You've been working for years in your police agency and starting to think more about the end of your police career. Some days, the routine, the shift work, and the office politics get you down. Read this book! It's full of inspiring and practical information about moving on to a second career.

Second Acts that Change Lives by Mary Beth Sammons (2009). This book is about following your heart and dreaming big dreams. Change careers and make the world a better place. Very inspirational.

The Job of Your Life by Karen Schaffer (2008). This is a very easy-to-read book that covers a wide range of employment topics. It's funny and entertaining but has a whole lot of very useful advice. Published by Sentor Media.

Jump Ship by Josh Shipp (2013). Isn't that a good title for a book about changing careers? I thought it was. He has a seven-step plan for getting to your dream job, all in a very down-to-earth writing style.

Second Career Volunteer by Barbara M. Traynor (2012). This one is different. It's all about volunteering your skills and time with an organization that fits with your experience. No pay. They provide room and board. You do volunteer work for them. You could have some great travel experiences this way and cut your costs.

Knock 'em Dead Resumes by Martin Yate (2014). This book includes a step by step method of examining the job you are applying for before you build your resumé. There are also one hundred resumés that actually worked for real applicants. A valuable asset in your second career search. Published by Adams Media, a division of F+W Media, Inc.

INDEX

Alboher, Marci 101
Analysis 44 – 55, 84, 89
ASIS International 72
Australian Job Outlook 92

Best Canadian Resumés 81
Bolles, Richard N. 93, 102
Building Blocks 29-45

The Career Change Resumé 81
Certified Fraud Examiner 60, 68
Certified Professional Resumé Writer (CPRW) 82
Certification(s) 60, 67-69, 72
Collamer, Nancy 93, 101

Develop a Plan 8, 14
Dolo, Tom 109, 96, 97
Dream Job 24, 25, 61, 62, 103

The Encore Career Handbook – How To Make A Living And A Difference In The Second Half Of Life 101
Encore – Finding Work That Matters in the Second Half of Life 102
Encore.org 101
Ewatski, Jack 11, 70, 98, 109

5 great ways to destroy your police career on social media 27
Five O'clock Club 93
Freedman, Marc 102
Gaps 65-74, 84, 86
Garcia, Ramon 95, 109

Gathering of Known Facts 6
Geary, Gail 102
Graham, Sharon 81

Hofferber, Karen 81
Human Resources and Skills Development Canada, Canadian Occupational Projection System (COPS) 91, 92

Investigator(s) 17, 27, 55, 76, 79
Investigation(s) 5, 6, 11, 13, 18, 24, 30, 36, 47, 48, 52, 57, 64, 65, 68, 75, 76, 79, 83, 84, 91, 95
Isaacs, Kim 81

The Job of Your Life 19, 103
Jones, Dave 69, 70, 109
Jump Ship 103

Knock 'em Dead Resumés 81, 104
Komisarjevsky, Chris 27, 102

Leadership 41, 52, 96
Levine, Mark 103
LinkedIn 71, 91, 98

MacLean's Magazine 2015 Guide to Jobs in Canada 92
Maddaloni, Michael V. 103
Management 16, 30, 41, 42, 45, 52, 92, 93, 99
McQuiggin, Kevin 15, 25, 68, 109
Membership(s) 60, 71, 72

National Association of Police Officers (NARPO) 91
Nationally Certified Resumé Writer (NCRW) 82
Network(ing) 60, 69-71, 90, 95, 100, 101
New Zealand Labor Market Information 92

Operational Plan (Ops Plan) 53, 74, 83, 85, 87, 89, 90, 92
Padar, Jay 16
Padar, Jim 16
Patrol 12, 16, 31, 35, 36, 38, 51, 59
Person of Interest 47, 55, 57, 58, 75
Person of Interest Report 57, 58, 62, 65, 74, 77, 84, 86
Police Academy 21, 34, 35, 36, 59
Pollan, Stephen M. 103
Polygraph Interviews 69
Portfolio 14, 28, 65, 66, 72-75, 84, 86, 102
The Power of Reputation 27, 102
Private Investigators' Association of BC (PIABC) 97
Private Security Industry 72
Professional Designation(s) 32, 60, 72
Profile 8, 19, 32, 47, 48, 71, 89

Qualification(s) 15, 35, 60, 65, 66, 68, 74, 77

Reputation 25-28, 59, 87, 102
Resumé 6, 8, 15, 58, 59, 64, 73-82, 84, 86, 93, 104
Resumé Format 80, 82

Sammons, Mary Beth 103
Schaffer, Karen 19, 103
Second-Act Careers 93, 101
Second Acts – Creating the Life You Really Want, Building the Career You Truly Desire 103
Second Acts that Change Lives 103
Second Career Plan 85
Second Career Volunteer 103
Security Consultant 70, 98
Self-assessment 22, 47, 101
Self-reflection 22

Shipp, Josh 103
Skill Analysis 47-55, 60, 65
Skill(s) 5, 11-15, 17-19, 24, 30, 32, 34, 38, 42, 44, 47, 51, 53, 55, 60, 65, 66, 68, 69, 76-79, 84, 86, 90, 96-100, 103
Social Media 26, 27, 98
Strengths 30, 32, 47-49, 53-55, 57, 60, 65-67, 77, 84
Supervisory experience 40

Thompson, Neil 100, 109
Traffic Accident Reconstruction Specialist 68
Training 11, 16, 21, 34, 36, 38, 40-43, 49, 55, 57, 59, 60, 66-70, 72, 73, 77, 87, 90, 94-96, 99
Transitions 103
Traynor, Barbara M. 103
Twitter 94, 98, 110

Volunteer 33, 42, 61, 96, 103, 104

Union, Police 42
U.S. Department of Labor, Bureau of Labor Statistics 91

Vaas, Lisa 82

Want To Research A Retirement Career? 93
Weakness(es) 30, 47-49, 54,55, 57, 60, 65, 66, 84
Weinblatt, Richard 27
What Color Is Your Parachute? - A Practical Manual for Job-Hunters & Career Changers 93, 102
WorkSafeBC 5, 17, 19, 27, 76, 79

Yate, Martin 45, 81, 93, 104
Your Next Career. Do What You've Always Wanted to Do 102

Acknowledgments

You might think people run in the opposite direction when asked to help with a book project. I was pleasantly surprised to learn that is not the case. In fact, I found just the opposite. I'm very thankful for the help and support I had writing this book.

All of the following offered valuable insight about moving from a career in law enforcement to a second career: Jack Ewatski, Kevin McQuiggin, Jim Padar, Dave Jones, Ramon Garcia, Tom Dolo, and Neil Thompson. I appreciate the time each of them took to tell me their stories.

Several friends read a draft of the book, and provided valuable feedback: Ken Bradley, Dale Djos, Andy Mendel, Brian McGuinness, Gord McGuinness, Kevin Murray, Bill Parsons, and Greg Ralla. Marilyn Olsen, president of the Public Safety Writers Association was very helpful with her detailed review. And it helps to have a brother who is a former high school teacher of English. My brother, Peter, read the manuscript twice and offered valuable comments on many writing points, for which I'm most grateful.

Anyone who has been a police officer knows there are times when you need some comic relief. Three cartoonists helped deliver the second career message in the book and kept us laughing too.

John Weiss is an artist, cartoonist, writer and Police Chief in Scotts Valley, California. I'm grateful for John's ongoing encouragement and support throughout this book project. His art work and blog can be viewed at johnpweiss.com.

Brad Hill is a Deputy Chief at the Evansville, Indiana, Police Department and a cartoonist as well. Brad has been a pleasure to work with and provided thoughtful insight from his years in law enforcement.

Mark Anderson is a professional cartoonist who lives in the Chicago area. His website, Andertoons, is at andertoons.com.

Others helped in a variety of valuable ways. Thanks to my niece, Susan Eldridge, Mira Thomas, Gary Sparks, Richard Dunn, Carol Schultz, Paul Gorton, Yushi Ebisawa, Akira Ebisawa, Barb Morris and John Unger.

My editor, Emmy-award winner Molly McKitterick, made the writing much more polished. She was fast, efficient, and helped me untangle the confusing parts.

Edward Wong of Vertex Design formatted the book and designed the cover.

My Twitter followers have been very encouraging. I'm grateful for their diverse and friendly advice.

Most importantly, my wife Lori has patiently lived with me through my police career, my second career, and this book project. I bounced many ideas off her and value her wise advice. As always, I'm grateful for her support!

Made in the USA
Columbia, SC
11 December 2017